Seeing 2020

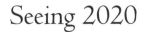

Pandemic :: Justice
Fire :: Election
Earth

poems from a big ye.

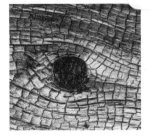

by Kim Stafford

Portland: Little Infinities
1 January 2021

copyright © 2020 Kim Stafford

These poems have appeared as they were written daily, together with photographs, at www.instagram.com/kimstaffordpoetry

"After Fire, Rain" appeared in the *New York Times*.
I wrote "In the Ash" after seeing a photo of Barry Lopez
    returning to the utter ruin of his writing studio.
"The Cardinal Debates the Jay" was inspired by the Middle
    English poem "The Owl and the Nightingale."
"Verbatim Transcript" is a verbatim transcript of the
    president's words.
The enigmatic words in "Election Oracle" are reported to have
    been uttered by the Delphic oracle in ancient times.

Two poetry films, with prompts for writers:
1. A poetry reading, with writing prompts:
    https://vimeo.com/412407427
2. A reading of pandemic poems:
    https://vimeo.com/414069499

Additional poems, films, workshops, and resources for teachers and writers can be found at www.kimstaffordpoet.com

Dr. Fauci's Smile, a book of earlier pandemic poems,
along with other collections of my poems for human need,
can be found by searching for "Kim Stafford" at www.lulu.com

Thanks to Bill Howe and Joy Bottinelli for supporting
this project, and other creative endeavors to raise the
human spirit through poetry.

Cover photo: Rosemary Stafford dressed for work on a
smoky day at the farm.

ISBN 978-1-716-26751-2

For the Children of Hard Times

Preface   In the early months of 2020 I was traveling to far-flung communities as Oregon's poet laureate, sharing the pleasures of language with students and teachers, writers and readers, immigrants, parents, veterans, inmates, and people living outside. When the pandemic put an end to these direct encounters in early March, I needed to hunker down and start sharing poetry online. I made two films for the twenty-five communities I had to cancel from my calendar, built a website to offer self-directed writing practice, and began posting poems as they were written every morning on Instagram. Because we were in lockdown, with no end in sight for the ravages of the pandemic, my writing practice shifted from "What do I want to write?" to "What do people need to read?" It felt like poetry needed to depart from art to become a kind of medicine—an elixir of words offering alternate perspectives, solidarity in the face of trouble, consolation, and when possible joy.

Then, as the year unfolded with the death of George Floyd, activism for justice joined the pandemic in our lives. My daily poems began to struggle with my country's long-standing enigmas of racism and denial. By summer's end, it was fires raging in the mountains that started to crowd my pages, a storm of flame and smoke scorching the homes of many, and prisoning everyone inside as toxic skies darkened for us all. Once fires waned, the fraught human hurricane of the election filled my days and sleepless nights. My Instagram hashtags ranged from #covid… to #breathe… to #smoke… to #vote.

What could I add as a writer to the frenzied news assaulting us each day? Every morning I walked the neighborhood in the dark, brooding over our troubles even as the birds began to wake and first light came. Then I sat in the presence of the latest news, felt in my heart and mind what hurt, inspired, or simply arrested me, and began to write, often beginning with a resonant word: responder…radical…ash…campaign….

One task of poetry may be to turn simple suffering into learning, hurt into empathy, confusion into reflection, and paralysis into resolve. I hope this book may sift from our common troubles some glimpses of opportunity for new ways to see our chance to live together on this fragile earth. If I begin with the question "How can I be a good citizen in a divided nation?" I sense the answer has a lot to do with respect, curiosity, listening, and kind connections. Seeking such answers, at one point I found myself writing a prescription for how to take a hardship, like the many this year has offered us, and school it into a lesson, and eventually a gift:

Schooling Sorrow

When a sorrow's young, it's pure—stunned
pang at breakup, betrayal, failure, death.
You weep, rant, brood, slump. And then

in the morning, sorrow starts its epic
journey into memory, becomes an island
in your archipelago of sufferings.

Then, if you are strong, and lucky to have
a listener—you begin to apprehend its quirks,
to tell it, shape it, watch it grow into a story.

And if you tell your story well, with curiosity
and courage, it then becomes a possession,
and in time a treasure, a smudge of wisdom.

This can be your gift, your offering—but
if you don't school your sorrow into story
it can never be your friend.

The book's last section holds poems for Earth, as that realm lies behind all we do. I offer this book as an album of recollections from 2020, and a prismatic meditation on how we might learn to be together beyond this year of struggle and hard learning.

Kim Stafford

Contents

5. Earth

I.

Pandemic

Woman Pumping Gas
Tells Me about the Crows

Through her pandemic mask, she confirms,
"Fill it? Regular? No receipt?" As her left hand
spins off the gas cap, her right slides home
the nozzle, and with a click the flow begins.
"See them?" She cocks her head to the power line,
where one crow cries, the other flaps and settles.
"That's the baby calling, not yet learned to fly."
Above the mask, her eyes look far. "I watched
all through June, July. Something got the others.
That one's left." We both look up at two silhouettes
against the sky. The gas hums. The young crow cries.
"My own girl's still home. Grown, but not gone.
Crow mama taught me: Give her time."
The gas valve clicks off. She holsters
the nozzle, spins tight the cap.
"You said no receipt?"

Game Changer

A virus we can't see has humbled us—
infinite terrorists crawling in a sheen on steel,
seething in the air, lurking on a knob, hitching
on a hand, then by the eye into the labyrinth of the self.

Economy becomes a house of cards. Politics a sorting game
for truth. Freedom, once our heritage and right, now
becomes our elusive goal. Can we surrender to confinement,
so someday thrive again?

Pandemic Post Office

Restricted hours for service.
Doors propped open so none touch.
People pivoting in retreat to pass.
The line marked at six-foot stripes.
Customers, clerks, all in masks.
Suspended plastic sheets to guard.
Yet we make our halting way
through this divisive labyrinth
to send connection far.

Installing a Sink
So Our Son Can Live Sequestered
in Our House for the Pandemic

I watch our four hands measure,
saw, drill, fit, hammer, tighten
the whole contraption of a kitchen
so we can live together apart
under this roof, so you can
come and go as you please.

Soon we will close that door,
you will be here, we there.
But now we crouch side by side
to prepare the magic of independence.

Water comes from far, born
of the sea, the sky, the mountain
to arrive at this tap you touch.
Then from here it goes in spiral
down the drain and away.

Your shoulder touches mine.

Home Improvement in the Pandemic

The hardware store is thick with dads
in masks prowling the plumbing aisle,
or fingering through pine planks,
or searching for a particular screw—
flat top, brass, no. 8, fine thread, Phillips—
or finally taking on that underground
watering system for the lawn with pop-up
sprinkler heads designed to fail.

The dad swarm keeps pouring in
from the parking lot, eyes gleaming
over their bandanas, each on a mission
of repair, or escape into the realm of fix.

We're lined up on our floor medallions
six feet apart, me with my PVC cement,
the next man with his copper pipe.
"Everyone's home breaking things,"
says one dad to the girl at the register
as he hands her a tangle of tools.
"That should bring you back," she says,
as she rings up his loot.

Our Next Big Thing

The deal-maker is in denial, Mr. Kentucky
on a tear, the zigzag death toll seeks the sky,
someone gets shot asking for a mask, a naming
party sparks another outbreak, the news is
mega fires and hurricanes, and our fears
come true like wishes turned to curses
that prey upon our foolishness.

So why does the wren still sing? Why
did I see a child skip, a mail clerk grin
in that moment she adjusted her mask?
Why the uptick in random kindnesses?
Dogs don't stop wagging, or flowers
opening their secrets. We must be
getting ready for the next big thing.

Last Responders

After rain quells fires our early heroes
could not stop, after heaped cardboard coffins
plunge into earth while kinfolk weep, after nurses
get paid in contagion for their troubles, and doctors
succumb to what they fought, after neighbors save
storm survivors, local volunteers giving all, after
drought in the heartland, flooding on the coast, long
after the news cycle has reported the latest shooting ,
hungry children, teeming jails, eviction epidemic, then
the last responders arrive, saying—from a safe distance,
from a podium dressed in flags, with a microphone
wiped clean—their trumped-up explanations and denials,
that what they can't see can't be real, that what they
can't solve can't be solved, that it's the American way
to recover on your own, be proud, remember the greatest
generation, wars we won, that we're the envy of the world,
that "Our hearts are with you…" before gathering their scripts,
shaking a few hands, making the most of every photo op,
bowing to climb into their black conveyances, tinted
windows gliding up, their motorcade gone
into the sunset's crimson pain.

Nurse's Note

When it began, you called us heroes—for facing down
the scourge, short on masks but long on determination
to honor every life from admitting to last breath.
You sang to us, you honked and spread our portraits
in the news just for doing our jobs.

You sang, yes, but you didn't change—instead,
by a rising epidemic of denial (you couldn't
mask, stay home, or forgo your festive habits
of wandering for pleasure), we were
finally overwhelmed.

Look into my eyes so I know you hear me.
You made us choose: give up our calling, or be
stricken on the job and die, leaving our children
weeping, alone, bitter with stories
of your fatal nonchalance.

Margie's Pie

Not the Halloween variety, but baking pumpkins smaller
than a soccer ball—take a batch to school and have the big kids
draw lovely faces, inviting eyes with lashes up in surprise,
a swoop of hair, the ear you see when a shy friend turns.

Take these faces to the younger kids, teach them to bowl,
one hand curled as you bow into pure intention, then knit
your body and quick step into the moment of release
when what was yours escapes along your line of desire.

Take these balls to the little ones to cradle in their arms
as they run relays back and forth across open ground,
everyone jumping and shouting as your receiver
opens her hands in welcome, ready for treasure.

At home, these pumpkins—split, seeded, steamed, scraped,
mixed with sugar and spice—will hold all that learning
and play, laughter and wonder baked into a pie. And when
the pie is opened, we begin to taste a better world.

Pandemicist

In every sort of trouble there will be those
who thrive: in famine, the hunger artist...
in fire season, the pyromaniac...in old age,
those of us given to a philosophic turn.

So in lockdown, may hibernators revel,
and introverts rejoice. Hermits never
had it so good—at dawn, silent bell the call
to prayer, and every hour an empty bowl.

2.

Justice

Knee to the Neck

Resist arrest...arrest the breath...cuff..
subdue...phone film review...gone viral...
protest spiral...oath to protect...knee to the neck...
let him breathe...check his pulse...a good man dies...
his mama cries...peaceful vigil...escalation...precinct
station jam-packed...ransacked...tear gas smoke...riot
woke...milk for eyes still on the prize...say his name...
chant his name...car in flames...who's to blame...riot gear
worn for fear...looting shooting...tweeting...beating...
call curfew...graffito scrawl...stun grenade...barricade...
justice arc...injustice spark...slave...brave...created
equal...brutal sequel...peace...police...release...
cities seethe for *I can't breathe.*

In Charge

A phone clip shot by a citizen takes command
of a nation, its searing blur sending orders
to far-flung forces marching day and night
in spite of beatings, tear gas, stun grenades,
and Black Hawk choppers hovering low.

Peaceful protest holds rare power over
crack-down when an old man, felled, is filmed,
or the swung club is caught on tape. Fires or looting
by a few can't blunt the momentum of the many
with their signs and singing, chanting a name.

For George—face down, eyes closed, breathless—
yet sends a human code that outranks a president,
no matter the bible in his hand upside down.
These are the times right makes might when, by their
national guardianship of honor, the people speak.

Counterfeit Twenty

The bill George Floyd paid for cigarettes,
a fatal fake, brought screaming squad cars,
an ambulance, a fire truck, films, then fires,
police in riot gear, the National Guard, curfew,
then jingle dress dancers to the drum at Chicago
and E. 38th—that bill should be displayed as relic,
talisman, emblem, icon revealing what's gone
down since slave ships sold lives for money
to divide brother from brother, sister from sister,
to thrust a knee to the neck of a father, husband,
mentor begging for simple breath. Twenty dollars?
Take one out and study it: Andrew Jackson with
the White House in the back of his mind, two trees
with no trunks, a twenty telling us we trust in God
by a serial number, telling us eight different times
it's a twenty just to be sure we know the worth
of a man's life and a nation's chance
to honor legal tender.

10 Generations

We are a young country on stolen land—
is it any wonder we still have much to learn?
Our anthem speaks of war—we are haunted
by our victories. Born by blood, we still think
guns and armies are the way to prevail. Is it
truth when you have to shout? Is it wealth
when you count by money? Are you free
when you think your only options
are liberty or death?

In Assisi, I met a man from Rome. "Your
country—200 years? When we were an empire
we thought we had to rule the world. Now,
we savor the pleasures of family, slow life,
and all that is beautiful. Your time will come.
Corragio!"

Law & Order

It's a law of motion: For every action
there will be an equal and opposite reaction.
When you bring more police, the protest will grow.
When you injure their children, mothers form a wall.
When you injure the idea that all are created equal,
the people seek to heal the injury. When you speak
with tear gas and stun grenades, it's in the natural
order of things that the people affirm their own
freedom to speak. And when the odd machine
of democracy drives the president to trade away
common sense for votes by the fearful,
it's time for an orderly change.

Protest Proposal

I'm standing here because I have a question,
not because I have an answer. I don't know
how policing should be done, but I know—
don't you?—how it should not. Can we agree
there might be better ways than choking,
beating, works of war? Can we agree a cop can't
be a cop and also a drug counselor, a social worker,
a teacher, an advocate for the homeless? Can we agree
a cop will be more successful as part of a team than as
a warrior facing the impossible? And if a mother
were at the table, a minister, a child, might the budget
be adjusted from hurt toward help?

At the Edge of What I Know
—for Jason Graham

In the epoch of pandemic and protest I escape
the prison of my certainties to breathe the open
sky. By dawn's early light, over my shoulder I
can see the glittering path of shackles where
they fell from some. Out from shadow, here in
sunlight, it's clear as day—going back to
normal would be the opposite of progress.
Up ahead, something better beckons for us
to imagine, design, and build, so we can
breathe the open sky.

What's Your Name?

"What's your name,?" my student
asked the officer at the protest line
after the command to disperse—

In response, this cop sprayed
my student's face, made him weep,
made me need to ask every badge,

"What's your real name?"

Weeds in Paradise

The lordly dandelion's sassy yellow?—
essential flight of lace-borne seeds.
Kudzu vine embracing a tree?—
gifted teacher for the climb
toward heaven. Stray thoughts
and forsaken plans?—matted
stuff of germination. Dissidents
in our democracy?—it's all
in how you see.

Change Dancer

After a night of street strife, the police chief
gives her televised press conference, and I want
to pay attention, but the signer beside her, a young
Black man in long sleeves and vest, is so expressive
her words become his ballet—and when she scowls,
he smiles, when she pauses he seems to levitate,
his wings about to open, as she speaks of the past,
a legacy of struggle, he signs the future,
unfurling his beautiful hands.

Headline

Retired Priest Performs Last Rites for Possum
on Highway then Creature Revives Restoring
Faith of Family Who Stopped to Watch Leading
Children to Years Later Study Zoology and Spend
Career Preserving Habitat for Endangered Species
Working in Collaboration with Local Residents
Resulting in Advocacy for Rural Poor Starting
with Access to Clean Water as Constitutional
Amendment for First Right of All Children
with Effort Joining Demonstrations in Cities
Chanting I Can't Breathe and Holding Up
Chalices Filled with Rain Causing Police
Chief to Remember Grandmother's Last
Wish that He Become a Teacher Causing
Order to Desist Confrontation and Begin
Dialog as Protesters Distribute Counterfeit
Twenty Dollar Bills with Image of George
Floyd and Motto *E Pluribus Pluribus* as
First Step toward Democracy of True
Inclusion in All Matters of Grace

Radical

Is it radical to seek for justice?
Is it radical to acknowledge the legacy
of slavery? Is it a revolutionary act
to stand your ground—not with a gun,
but with a question: How shall we be
a better nation?

It's radical to send agents to maraud
citizens. It's radical to design distractions
when a crisis is at hand. It's the wrong
revolution when voting is suppressed,
and civil strife encouraged.
Such is not my country.

Going back to our roots, we seek
that all are equal...where speech is free...
in a more perfect union...so we can know
domestic tranquility.

National Vocation

What is our Calling? What are We the People
now called to Believe, to Envision, and to Do?
If we are the new Founders of a better Nation,
what do we Declare, and how shall we Constitute
an America more True to our old Aspirations of late
Educated to a new Clarity: true Equality, non-abusive
Liberty, and Happiness in keeping with all Creatures
of the Earth? These are again the Times that Try our Souls,
but now the Tyranny we battle is Complacency, Denial,
machinery of Greed and Power inimical to our Common
Good and future Prospects. If Preamble to our new
Covenant has been Drought, Fire, Storm, and Pestilence,
shall we now Elect ourselves to be bold Patriots of Children—
their Chance, their future Happiness, their World in Balance?
In place of *Give me Liberty or give me Death*, I propose
May the Young not Perish from the Earth.

The Secret behind Our Strife

I, so sure of myself, so ready
to explain why I am right—
I live in a body that will die, and all
my brave words be gone to the sky.

And you, with your shouted reasons
I am wrong, you live in a body
that will fall, be still, be mourned
for the peace you might have found.

Shall you and I, knowing this now,
set our strife aside, shift our proclamations
into curiosity, listening to see what we
might learn, one from another?

3.

Fire

Smoke in Oregon

It comes from somewhere I can't see
to brush soft fists against the window,
filter through cracks and pinch my breath—
rolling in to rouse me with hard news
from lost trees at Opal Creek, from homes
now ash in Detroit, Mill City, Molalla.
It drives prisoners from their cells,
the infirm from their hospitals,
children from their known world.
Roads are headlight tunnels, towns
rocked by lockdown and evacuation.

We burned the oils of ancient leaves
to drive our chariots ever faster, to heat
the sky like there was no tomorrow.
Now we live in tomorrow's ghost
where the sky kindles everything.

When the wind shifts and skies clear, when
rain falls, how shall we change for remedy?
What has all this smoke now clarified?
Who did this to us? Head hung low,
through smoke I raise my hand.

In the Ash

Blunt stump where the tree stood.
Hulk and melted metal of a car.
Concrete steps to charcoal floors.

Where the door, knob and hinges.
Where the wall, a path of nails.
Where the window, shattered shards.

Where room, rectangle of debris.
What shone, or blazed with color,
now dressed in tarnish and rust.

Our blessing? No bones.
In this box of sky, at least
we weep together.

Holy Smokes

Downwind from where the forest burns
we inhale the cindered souls of trees
that in a whoosh became particulate
and rode the wind to enter us. With
this breath take in the spirit whisker
of a mouse, incincerate wren's cry
clenched and tumbled from the sky,
moss that leaped from green to nothing,
flailing leaf that in a fiery gasp
rushed through charcoal into dust
inside the billow flame that roiled and—
holy, holy, holy became the smoke-smudge
pall that smuggled mountains into us.

Now freighted for life with dusky mist,
even as we help sustain our neighbors
who lost everything but life, we survivors
are the walking shrine of little lives. We are them,
are earth mind suddenly, to weigh by human choice
what's best for upward yearning seed of cedar,
footfall of the mouse, wingbeat of the wren.

Distant Fires

Far to the south, to the east, trees burn—
fields, barns, houses. Wind brings us smoke,
a rumor of flame, of black earth, of suffering.
We study the sun smudge, almost hear high
in our uneasy trees a roar of heat,
shout of mother, shriek of horse.

Will the capricious eye of sorrow rove
to find us, grief storm seeking new ground?
Distance is our fiction, safety our illusion
as hard news travels like the wind, hungry
to be rooted with us, too, to turn our
ordinary days into tough history.

Inmate Fights Fire

When it gets really bad, they want me out—out there
on that fire-line, sweating sparks, staring down flames
I look up to as I dig like some fiend. Dollar an hour
to be a crispy critter to save somebody's home. Yeah, they
figure the same jinx of brave and stupid got me convicted
might make me right to stand my ground for fire.

Like these boots? Like this hickory handle I flick
back and forth so my shovel slashes dirt, leaves
no food fire can eat? I like leaning back to see
that red sun staring through these skeleton trees
like bars in my cellblock window. And the wind
brings me smoke for free. Free?

When my sentence ends, you think I'll walk free?
You think they'll look at me to say, "He's good"?
They plot their own fire-line to keep me on the dark side.
Got it? Like my face tattoo says "Bad Man. Don't Hire."
You can walk out the prison gate, but try walking through
the reputation wall to freedom after they call you felon.

I served my time. Serious good behavior. And after?
Give me a chance. Or shall I say, *I've been burned.*

Fire & Seed

Fire can't burn stone, would starve
without dry texture, filament fine,
a thicket, a ladder of sticks climbing
toward the sun—and this the seed provides.

Seed can't grow, would stay below
in darkness without some sky, bare
ground rich in sunlight for reveling
open and up—which yellow flame provides.

And what of us with our fields, barns,
and houses burned when fire rides
the wind down the canyon into town?
Shall we lose everything to learn?

We need each other now.
Old tree, send down your seeds.

Oregon Burning

A hundred houses, two hundred,
with only few lives snuffed out—
how does that happen? It's called
heroes, miracles of right action:
fist-hammered doors at midnight.
Get out. Take nothing. Now!

West with the wind, a caravan creeps
down the canyon, each driver's eyes
lit red by fire in the rearview mirror.
Blue River gone, Finn Rock, Nimrod,
Vida…Idahna, Detroit, Mill City…
Talent, Phoenix…the little towns of home.

Chimney built to hold the fire stands solo
over charcoal rubble all along the street
of smoking trees, treasures a dark stain
on bare earth. Fire took everything—except…
except the story of who we are, and will be,
when we circle for home, after the rain.

After Fire, Rain

The soft smoke of hard rain
drilling down through tree bones.
The hiss and steam of quenched fire—
rain nipping flame's root, gray mud of ash.
Rain walking up the canyon, reaching down
for every stem reaching up, dressing wounds.
Sound of rain slapping your hat. Rain gloves.
Rain making your coat heavy, your neck cold.
Boots leaving prints in mud, signature of rain.
Rain washing what was seared, culled, fallen, lost.
Where fire fed, rain offering food, rest, restoration.
Rain turning eye-salt to rivulets, rivulets
to rivers wheresoever many weep as one.
After fire, rain offering a few true words.
Rain thrust deep in earth, seeking seeds.
Rain in haste, eager rain, patient rain,
rain taking its own sweet time.
Earth's thirst for first rain—
never to be cursed again.

After

To haunt the old life, a survivor stands where the door stood
to survey what once was house—gray rectangle of ash, twisted
pipe, bricks and cinders, then steps in to sift for remnants,
for a spoon, a key, to all that's lost, a hammer, tools
to start the restoration. At least something precious
for the children.

To seek the old ways, I stand in the ruins of my country,
a map-shape hollowed by division and strife. I, too, would
sift for remnants I could use to restore the family, taking up
a tarnished "We the people…," a rusty "In many, one…,"
and twisted almost beyond recognition, "In order to form
a more perfect union…."

Here, take a shovel with me. Maybe we can find "Give me
your tired…," and "I have a dream today." Maybe we could
polish old words like *Ask what you can do for your country*
until they work again, so we could not be at war with the world
and ourselves, so we could insure domestic tranquility
by listening, wondering, honoring.

Friend, can you help find something shining for the young?

Sweet Air

Wind shifted, then rain came,
our smoke drifted east and south,
the sun's medallion went from red
to yellow, the far horizon cleared,
and from their dark dens the people
came forth squinting at the sky.

Midnight, waking, your window open
for the first time in weeks, you taste
the sweet, almost painful
breath of trees delving deep
into your being, saying softly,
Now you have been warned.

Now your work is listening to voices
magnified by tragedy. Now you send
your listening up into the dark. High
against the stars, geese call, rowing south
as they gaze down on the scattered lights,
the restless map of our human catastrophe.

Where There's Smoke

On the east coast, hurricane.
On the west coast, fire.
And in between, denial.

In the air in Oregon, smoke.
In the forecast, more. And for
our children's lives, "You can't
change the weather" is a lie.

Coming soon, an election.
Coming after, with either outcome,
the hardest work we've ever done.
So what can each one do?

Be the cooling trend you want to see.

4.

Election

Whisper & Sing

Blunt shouts we have plenty, and
abundant silence about hard things.
There are many who talk the talk, and
dog whistle innuendo is everywhere.
But a mother's whisper to a child's
bright eyes? Or the murmur of a friend
at moonrise? Or that time in Wales
when fifty strangers in the bus station
began to sing in harmony—one voice,
then two, then everyone? That's
the world I want.

Can My People Be All People?

*I believe in. . .an aristocracy of the sensitive,
the considerate, and the plucky.*
                              —E.M. Forster

My kin, my kind, my enemy, my friend—how
does it all add up? "It takes all kinds to make a world,"
my father said—"but there's an oversupply of some."
For every kindred soul, there are the others, greedy, arrogant,
lonely in their fury, a sort only God, on a good day, could love.
Could I love them into change? Could I see a father in a man
with a club, a daughter in a woman armored in diamonds and
fur, a frightened child in a tyrant's swagger? Could I seek
connection, find new ground where we could begin again?
And what are they to make of me, a poet with more dreams
than plans, prone to judgment, prisoner of ideals? One way
or another, or another, or another, can we sort this through?

Think Twice

If you think once, that's good—
you're ahead of the game. But do
yourself a favor, and think again.

Think for yourself, for number 1.
Then think for others, and see
how you are woven into we.

Think for today, necessity.
Then think for what comes soon,
and after, all that rich unfolding.

Think for your allies, then for "enemies."
Think for the human, then for Earth.
Think for comfort, then for deepening spirit.

When anyone demands an answer, say,
"I am of two minds. Give me a moment."

Evolution of the Campaign Promise

I alone can fix it.
I can use my great wisdom
to direct others to fix it.
We could sit down together and I
could lead us to figure out how to fix it.
Maybe we could start by listening
to the future, and work backward
to do what the children need us to do.
How about we empower the children,
and work for their long well being?
Let's start by saying we've been wrong
about many things, but because we
now rely on everyone in the human project,
we have a chance to make things right.
Tell me—how can I help you all
to repair the world?

The Democrats Wager Everything
on the Human Story

The Convention was unconventional, all
online, many-voiced, listening to the People—
to a stuttering child, a grieving wife, to sisters,
farmers, former first lady, last survivor, dreamer,
veteran, laborer, immigrant, sufferer uninsured,
laid-off worker, listening to the voiceless voiced,
the old, the young, the honored dead.

The rich and powerful had their say—
warnings from the billionaire, from
political rivals become allies, from
celebrity actor, music star, governor,
senator, and former president—but
true resonance spoke to us from
the unknown faithful and the good.

When we vote, they asked us all,
shall we trust the people? Is it true,
from the many, we are one?

Questions Prior to Debate

How are you? And your family?
I've been watching you carry yourself—
and I can relate. It's heavy these days.
And it's no picnic growing old.
We both know, once we begin
they'll judge our every word.
Can we agree there's much to do
to make our people safe and well?
For you, what makes you curious
in these mysterious days? What
have you been learning? If we
disagree, could we still be fellow
citizens, still be patriots of a different
persuasion? End of the day, what do we
want for the children, for the long future?
What do we fear? How can we help?
What shall we face together?

Now we know a common goal,
let's debate the best way forward.

The Cardinal Debates the Jay

The crimson Cardinal perched
on the topmost branch of a twisted
pine, the Bluejay a bit below,
and they both fluffed their feathers.

"This top branch is mine to keep,"
the Cardinal said—"your flock
of riffraff can't change that. And if
they try, we'll ask the owls."

"I believe in the long migration,"
the Bluejay said—"in a different
time to come. Have you given
no thought to the fledglings?"

"You and your far horizon,"
the Cardinal said. "I believe
in this branch now—so beautiful!
Everything else—rumors and lies."

"Look down," the Bluejay said. "Oh
say can you see the sparrow, towhee,
nuthatch, flicker, heron, thrasher, swan,
the raven, crow, the robin and the wren?"

Accountability

Count the vote of the one who died,
and of the one left weeping.
Count the sister staring far,
then the child trying to sleep.
Count the doctor leaning
on her arms, the nurse who
bent close for the last breath.

Count how many will delete
a phone number, then remember
who they need to call—the good
listener, kind friend, dear heart gone.
Only by a census of the disappeared
can we represent our people
when we cast our ballots now.

Verbatim Transcript
[with questions from the people]

I'm feeling better now. We're working hard to get me
all the way back. I have to be back because we still have to
make America great again.

*[Mr. President, can you tell us how Hope is doing, or
Chris...?]*

Therapeutics are miracles. People criticize me when I say that.
Miracles coming down from God.

[Has this made you think about the thousands...?]

I want to thank the leaders of the world for their condolences.
They know what as your leader I have to go through.

[Now shall we wear masks, shall we avoid...?]

I had to be out front and this is America, this is the United
States, this is the greatest country in the world, this is the most
powerful country in the world.

[Now that the virus has touched your circle...]

I can't be locked up in a room upstairs, totally safe,
and just say 'Hey, whatever happens happens.'

[What can you say to those who still don't have...?]

We have to confront problems. As a leader you have to
confront problems.

[Mr. President...]

So that's where it is.

D.C. Weather Report

It's now clear the times they are a-changin':
the cold front that arrived some years ago
shows signs of breaking up in the coming weeks
as a new weather system moving in from all directions
has gathered in tornado alley and the Bible belt,
where the clouds have parted, and visibility improved.
This generally happens when the barometer drops
and stale air is freshened by incoming winds. Stubbornly,
the storm's eye remains fixed on capitol hill, where
observers have noted an air of preternatural calm
that long-time weather watchers know can be fickle.
Throughout the country, local residents are still repairing
storm damage from previous events, from fires creating
their own weather, from drought, from wind-shear episodes
of Stormy Daniels, ICE damage, and a surge of evictions
despite the fabled Operation Warp Speed. At least for now,
Hurricane Melania remains stalled off the coast, but may
make landfall soon, though evacuations orders have been
put on hold. Stay tuned. As you can see by our satellite
weather map, when viewed from above the whole country
is gripped by unsettled conditions, shifting trends, where
from California to the Gulf Stream waters, this land
is due for atmospheric change. Forecast: windy
late in the day, with an overnight low.

Under Oath

Your Honor, before I touch that Bible—very nice Bible,
by the way, could we clear something up? The *truth*?
I'm supposed to swear to that…but it's fake news,
everywhere. Ask anyone. These days, who can find a dollar
in a dustbin? People say good luck with that. As for
the *whole* truth, are we living in the past here, some
kind of virtue Disneyland? I know some people believe…
you can read about it. Nothing *but* the truth? If you can't
find a nickel, your Honor, you can't find a dime. Could we
skip this part, and get on with the show? A very fine doctor
says I have this disability—can't tell the difference. Can I
tell you about my father…there was a time I wanted…
but you know how it goes when money comes into it.
Truth, whole truth, nothing but…your Honor, wish
I could, but someone didn't do their homework
if they thought I could swear to that.

Election Oracle

In ancient Greece, the mighty took their questions
to the Oracle at Delphi—a poor woman who
could not write her name, but in a smoky trance
would prophesy:
Your statues shiver with dread...
Danger from a herald in scarlet...
Drown your spirits in woe...
Better the stranger....
She gave guidance by enigma chanted wild
as she slumped above her chasm muttering
wisdom deeper than the wise.

Now, we trust numbers with our fate
in a frenzy of counting until the count controls
our future, but does not explain. Oracle,
we beg you to be clear.
You ask too much...pray to the winds...

Trusting the Election

If you can't trust the final outcome, maybe
you don't trust the news reporters' numbers.
Are they on your side? Or maybe you don't trust
election workers who did the count. Did they
have skin in the game? Or can't you trust judges
who certified? What do they know of your life?
Or maybe it's the voters you don't trust, millions
who had their say. Have they seen your struggles,
helped with the rent, given your kid a break?
Or is it the constitution you don't trust, dusty
document from back in forever—what did those
founding fathers know about your nights
turning over fevered troubles in your mind?
Or does it go deeper, closer to home—you can't
trust what life will be when things change?
Who's going to care about you, anyway, all
those others so smug with their big share?
Or maybe you can't trust yourself—to manage
this life without a big guy saying, "Trust me."

Rogue Lame Duck

Snug in bunker, hunkered down, sunk
in fury and regret, feasting on bread baked
in the rumor mill—how many truths
can one lie kill if it's big enough to quell
all doubts, beyond the shadow of a certainty?
Off the rails, out of bounds, in the rough—
power mixed with fear can start the countdown
like a fuse sparking toward inauguration,
your executive branch bent on executions,
pardoning those who plea by promising
undying loyalty to a lost cause now bent
on destruction by neglect, Commander AWOL
 retreating, tweeting, dreaming, scheming for
one last fleeting rush before even a tower
and a wall are not enough protection from
the rising sea of troubles you are heir to
when the people choose another.

Do Your Job

If you are a farmer, you have married
weather—for hotter or for colder,
for wetter or for drier, unto death.
Do you weary? It's your job.

If you are a miner, you take on
the hero's journey into earth,
tunneling the deep dark.
Do you fear? It's your job.

If you are a trucker, you sleep
somewhere beyond the far horizon
by a song with eighteen wheels.
Are you homesick? It's your job.

If you are a president, you gather
the wise, learn what is, honor truth,
and do what must be done.
Is it hard? It's your job.

Key to a History Vocab Quiz
for the Next Century

Fraud = honest judgment.
Executive Tweet = evidence for a diagnosis.
McConnellist = patriot of party. Giuliani Factor =
high shenanigans spun in circles. Linsy Gramsie =
a weathervane. The Trump-Fauci Scale = a measure
for human character. Oxygen of Democracy = news.
Fake News = inconvenient truth. Big Beautiful Wall =
paranoia. Red Meat for the Base = a diet hard on the heart.
'Fake' & 'Hoax' = four-letter salt & pepper seasoning
for a rally. White House Bunker = a location for executive
pouts between rounds of golf. Pardons & Executions =
last act in a dark drama.

Bonus terms: beautiful call, China virus, medical cocktail,
positive test, anti-masker, dog whistle, good people on
both sides. Stormy, Mueller, Comey, taxes under audit,
Mar-a-Lago, sharpiegate, Say Her Name, Proud Boys,
Antifa, BLM, ICE, RBG, MAGA, stand down/
stand by, pandemic, stimulus, stop-gap,
The Great Healing of 2021.

The Fauci-Trump Scale
of Human Character

I. Seeing a child weeping alone, would you:
   a. bow down to ask what's wrong...
   b. shout for the parents...
   c. call ICE.

2. Seeing hospitals filled by Covid, would you:
   a. address the community about how to help...
   b. put on your mask and lie low...
   c. pout.

3. Seeing facts that contradict your hopes,
   would you:
   a. learn...
   b. linger...
   c. lie.

4. Seeing you have failed to achieve
   a cherished outcome, would you:
   a. move on...
   b. spin the story...
   c. golf.

I Have Voted

I have voted, said smoke from flaming trees
sending dark opinions with the wind. And I,
said hurricanes Hanna to Zeta—we've cast our
roving eyes across tattered maps. I voted,
gasped the last breath when knee pressed neck
and poured the people into streets of strife.
Every ventilator—switched off—was a vote,
every mass-grave cardboard coffin was a vote,
every child staring at a screen for school.
Every lie spoken from on high, every denial
was a vote for change. Every songbird
struck from the sky, pelting desert earth
to be counted was a vote. It all adds up,
catastrophe a landslide any way you tally.
So we are citizens electors representing Earth.

Draft for the Third Inaugural

Years later, in the Presidential Library,
filed under "Shred," they found scribbled
in sharpie on the backs of hotel stationary
a document one historian has called
the smoking gun of a faltering coup:

Some of the people of the red States,
in order to spark a more corrosive division,
jeopardize justice, disrupt domestic tranquility,
endanger the common defense, injure
the general welfare, and limit the blessings
of liberty to our personal allies and their
posterity, do proclaim and decree
executive privilege for the
President of America.

The Archivist has filed these pages
in a growing division of the collection:
"Unconstitutional."

Notes for a Granddaughter's
Presidential Inauguration, 3001

In the quarter century since our nation's
tri-centennial, and our new covenant....

For some years now, we have measured
economic success by the weather.

Now that justice listens to the poor....

In some schools, as you know, the whole
curriculum is trees.

Now that the custom wanes, we
can ask, "Why so many prisons?"

Cars back then, with their long trails
of blue smoke....

I can now report our work in mending glaciers....

At last we can speak with joy of what
our children will inherit.

Be a beekeeper.

Winter Solstice 2020

Once the sun is gone to rest, just at dusk
before the longest night, the deepest dark and
sharpest cold, when we're swung from summer
far, look west to find the Great Conjunction,
Saturn's spin aligned with Jupiter, conjoined,
twin lights one that beckons to the wise.

Oh my enemy, my rival, my neighbor on this Earth,
why don't our children know each other's names?
Might pandemic, protest, fire, and toxic politics
teach us what we need from one another, how
this turning bends our orbits closer for the arc
of justice, which is ours to welcome, to align?

Come 2080, when you and I are gone, when
the Great Conjunction comes round again, shall
our children say, "They failed us all—they left no
beauties to us, only strife"? Or might they say,
"Peace was never perfect, but they brought
their little lights together to make the many one."

5.

Earth

Apprentice to the Rain

Ancient bounty, show how it's done—every drop
a sip, a gift, a vote spattering stone, darkening earth
in the long election of the good. Teach us your trick
of quiet majesty where all opposition falls away
when the offering is pure. In many, one—a perfect
union, you clean the mountain, comb the valley, brim
the desert spring. Your quest is thirst, your means
of travel mist, blessing our survival. While we hoard
old opinions, for and against, you fall in all the hills,
rivulet the hollows, gather as you go, and never
says the river "That's enough."

Deep State

You can't see what's really going on,
can't know how it's really all controlled.
It came before you—old, strange, hidden
below the surface, behind the light.

There are clues, if you choose to read:
drought, fires, rough weather, rising seas.
Roots of grass, odyssey of thistledown,
butterfly migration, whale song.

In the foreground, a frenzy of humans,
puppets without strings who can
barely nudge the deep state this way
or that—but in the end are all

in thrall to fire, wind, and rain.

Pantheon

We live an ancient story: if we offend
the spirit of the Sky, sending high our smoke
of haste, fire will punish everyone. If we offend
the spirit of the Waters, ice will melt, seas rise,
storms will lash the coast—flood here, drought there,
and all will suffer. If we offend the spirit of the Earth,
spring will be consigned to hell, birds die, crops wither.

Call this mythology? Say it's just a story? Say
you have a better explanation? You're talking
to yourself, while the people thirst and burn,
while the children beg for better stories.
Our suffering is logical and real, and remedy
is clear: sacrifice the Wall Street bull of endless
greedy growth, and live a simpler life.

Wild Bird Sings in the City

I prefer trees that plant themselves
in back alley cracks in concrete
for a slice of tall noon sun.

I prefer to nest in shadows,
to be heard but not seen,
to feast on seeds and rain.

Before dawn, I prefer vast silence
hungry for a small song. When you
stand still, and turn to look up,

I am for you with a few true syllables.

Aspen

We dug a knee-high sapling twig
east of the mountains to set in city earth
beside our house, brought water to its tenderness
and watched first leaves unfurl and tremble.

Then this morning, kneeling on the lawn,
I see a dozen sprouts scattered where our little tree
has planned a grove, sending roots to reach and rise,
all one being, a myriad urge, a forest surging up.

Little aspen, wrinkle the ground.

Background

For city people, the foreground gleams,
hums, and promises with numbers, words,
images, and assistance with haste.
In the background, far away, someone
is making food and gizmos to fill the foreground
with distracting comforts.

For country people, the foreground sprouts
grows, and blossoms with color, fragrance,
fruit, and assurance of plenty.
In the background, far off,
someone is making news and money
to crowd the foreground with apprehension.

For crickets, wrens, and foxes
the foreground is all: crumpled grass,
rain, flicker shadow, blood and bone,
smoke, crevice, nest, deep den,
scent, starlight, thicket, moon,
dawn, longing, rustle, yip.

Under My Breath

As by dark I wandered,
the white-hot full moon
punched me in the eye,
and tall stars slid
their needles into my
upraised arms praising
what illuminates, as crickets
chanted psalms from shadows
so ravishing in small I had to
whisper with them, be their animal,
and silence pouring from the dark
ravine hit me like a wave
deafening my defenses
until I was a rag.

All these earth beauties
hammering my heart, is it
any wonder I can't live forever
if such pleasures bruise me
every night?

Raccoon in Plum Time

You live in a hollow tree—with bugs. In rain,
you drag heavy—coat and tail soggy where
the streetlights glitter. You watch your paws
soften scraps in a muddy puddle, making do
with what you find—peel, bone, rind.
Every street could be your last—headlights
hunting you flat. Then dogs—send you up a tree
for laughs, they'll sit there bragging as if they're
wolves. And you can only steal so much
cat food, scattered stinking underfoot before
you gag. What's abundance, if it's vile?

But then September, big moon, and your prowling
finds the plums dropping in heaps so sweet and fat
you stagger deep, whiskers quivering to lick, suck,
gnash, and swallow until you're sticky, lolling tipsy,
bandit happy, lusty gusto, shaky elbow, roly poly
on your side helpless with joy.

All those rainy nights of cold to come—
you'll remember plum time.

Fatherland, Motherland, Childland

We're sorry we couldn't leave you the butterflies,
but we were in haste. They were such a lovely decoration.
And the bees, well—we learned to synthesize their honey
from oil so you could taste as you listen to their digital,
atavistic hum. As for the birds—we have preserved
their colors on this screen—tap a hue to hear a song.
And whales, we have a whole library of their moans
which became utterly beautiful as their numbers dwindled—
rivaling, some say, any human music. We still have geology,
more visible with every passing year, the story of earth
revealed in seam and stratum. Out of our love, we saved
all these exhibits, just for you.

Fulcrum

In the vast Calder mobile of the world
the hummingbird flies up at the far tip
that's balanced by the blue whale diving
deep, and we, our fingers everywhere,
wreaking havoc with the balance
on which we all rely.

My Climate Accord

If I can't sign my own, what will my country's signature
mean? How could we ever prosper in the end? So…

Whereas I have been eating trees felled to make farms
to feed me, and sawdust grows bitter in my mouth;

Whereas reefs bleach so I can drive where I please,
my car cooking the sky, my errands smoking heaven;

Whereas the ice of eons calves and crashes, sending
high seas to every coast so I can spend, consume, discard;

Whereas the wild withers, earth erodes, songbirds starve,
and all the little lives wane for my convenience;

I therefore sign this covenant, here in the green grove
of young trees, at the tomb of the unknown child.

Stranger in the House

I was a stranger in the house of Earth—
broke the door, insulted the family,
never learned the language
beyond *want...mine...now...*,
slept in the best room, scattered
my debris, kicked the dog,
never fed the cat, threw out
the children's toys.

Once I was gone, they all
looked at each other, surveyed
the damage—sheen of oil, bones
of whales, dusty drought. They
shook their heads, and someone
said, "What was that about?"

Earth Graffiti

Even in Eden the ancient urge—
Eve chiseling E in petroglyph,
and Adam with his flake of flint
whittling A to make bark bleed.

Now we do it bigger: calligraphic
asphalt cloverleaf scribing farmland
with swooping signatures of speed,
cursive snarl of wires across the sky,

every city a tag for the human gang
saying *this our turf,* until the whole
round Earth wears spray paint tattoo,
enigma shout applied by the blind.

Good-Hearted

You can have a bad heart—be old, feeble,
fragile, and slow—and still be good-hearted,
still have a disposition to be awake, dressed
in a light children can sense, dogs can trust,
horses recognize. Reach your fearless open
hand across barbwire at the field's edge
and the pony's nose will yearn to you,
huffing and taking in your trusted scent.

How did you get to be this way?
I was lucky.
How can I find your luck?
Be kind.

Here and There

Here—in the realm of the living—we struggle
when we disagree, and truth is hard to find.
There—in dreams or imagination or after death—
it may be easier to know, to say, and to do.

Here, we stagger labyrinths of shouting,
lies, and fears, of hungers never satisfied.
There, those we lost are waiting with
simple words and long embrace.

Is this a time to hurry, then—to exit
our days of trouble for some dawn beyond?
Or shall we relish struggle far into age,
and freight our souls with sorrows rich

and strange to carry beyond the border, puzzle
our possession, and pain our lullaby for sleep?
I say taste every seed of the pomegranate,
forsaking none, not the bitter nor the sweet.

Old Beginning

Dawn is an ancient custom
we loved when we lived in trees:
smudge, glimmer, flash and shine.
And long under starlight would we
crouch by water for the new moon's rise:
crescent boat restless on the waterskin.
We learned to kindle new fire
with an old ember kept alive
by smoked root in a hollow bone.
When the dark season turns, days
begin to lengthen, long lost birds
return, and seeds ache open,
again we suffer our old rebirth. So,
on this new year's day primordial,
may old wisdom serve young days.

I January 2021

Kim Stafford is a writer in Oregon who teaches and travels to raise the human spirit. He is the author of a dozen books of poetry and prose, including:

Having Everything Right: Essays of Place
The Muses Among Us: Eloquent Listening
    and Other Pleasures of the Writer's Craft
Early Morning: Remembering My Father,
    William Stafford
Wind on the Waves
We Got Here Together
Entering the Grove
Prairie Prescription
How to Sleep Cold
Wild Honey, Tough Salt
Singer Come from Afar

In May 2018 he was appointed Oregon Poet Laureate for a two-year term by Gov. Kate Brown.

CPSIA information can be obtained
at www.ICGtesting.com
Printed in the USA
BVHW070759030321
601494BV00006B/522